Tangled Yarn

Rebecca Wasil Sheppard

BookLeaf Publishing

India | USA | UK

Presentation by *BookLeaf Publishing*

Web: www.bookleafpub.com

E-mail: info@bookleafpub.com

ISBN: 9789360943530

First edition 2024

To my stardust.

A Love Letter to an Alternate Reality

Twist
Stab
Hook
Grab
Pull.
Sinew. Fibers. Tubes. Clinging to foreign tissue.
It doesn't belong.
Aching deep. Aching a little less. An ache never
fully realized.
Tangled organs.
Tangled yarn.
Fingers rub aimlessly,
breathing—something—into what was once
nothing.
A something never actualized.
Nesting for someone else.
Scars deep inside. Real from disease. White
from age.
Seen on photographs. Scars deeper; "invisible."
Not so sensical.
"Get your vaccine," they cry.
"It was too late," I say.
"Get your pap," they sigh.
"I did. For 15 years," whispered in dismay.

Imperfect booties for a baby soon to be born.
Made by hands that will never bear children of
her own.

Bluebird

"Namu namu," hands clasp in prayer,
chopsticks handled carefully over a bowl of
steaming rice.
Thankful for the meal and hesitantly, eagerly
watching
each sticky grain travel
from wooden bowl gripping the chopstick
soaring through the air toward a gaping and
eager mouth.

"No, I do not need help."

"Namu namu," uttered under his breath as he
steps
forward into summer.

*"Namu"
[1] A word used to express devotion to Buddha
or the Three Treasures. Katsukazu Tsunegisho
(611) Ichijo Akira "Ichinomunamure hei ni more
zenichi"
[2] [[Impressed.]] 1) Words uttered when asking
someone for help. Miscellaneous Haiku

Yangitaur Shui (1801) Volume 9 "Namu's Wife Chichi Comes in Her Own Body" 2) Words uttered when taking a bold action without thinking deeply. Shinsen Osaka Poetry Encyclopedia (1841) "Namu means he does things without hesitation"

Bluebird 2

5

"Namu namu," hands grip in prayer,
chopsticks handled warily over a bowl of tepid
rice.
Thankful for the meal yet wearily watching
each sticky grain travel
from plastic bowl grasping the chopstick
traveling through the air toward a hungry mouth.

"Yes, I do need help."

"Namu namu," uttered under his breath as he
steps
forward into summer.

Serpent's Lament

Skin flakes off wholly
Unmasking as lady's gloves and women's
hosiery
Taken off after an evening show.

Shedding happens so rarely.
Shedding happens so frequently.
During times of growth
During times when I am too much.

I am no caterpillar transmuted
Into primordial ooze
Emerging later as a butterfly.

She's a serpent.
Never once donning the visage of purity.
Eden and Eve on Broadway and 180th Street.
Am I power and potential,
Fierce and to be feared?

Or am I Ouroboros,
Forever chasing my tail,
Devouring myself and no real substance.

A Tuesday At Two

Brimstone coursing
Pulsing just beneath the surface
It smells of onions.
There are no onions.

Spears of icicles stinging,
tentacles never releasing.

Electricity emulsifying
My very neurons
Changing words into ash.

Volcanic screaming
Releasing from my every pore.

Moss & Crack

A microcosmic forest grows
in the crack of our sidewalk,
Shades of lemony moldavite
against the piss and blood-stained concrete.

I search for this sign of life
Persistent despite the desperate
Drug-addled delusions
of a 4 a.m. skeletal huddled mass
shadowed in our neighboring stoop.

The damp, earthy sponge
soaking up nutrients where no other would seek
Exists in such contrast to my witching hour
comrade
who pushes poison into any vein she can find.

The crevice goes days, weeks looking dusty.
The stoop, too, abandoned.

Then, it rains.

My miniature crevasse comes back to life
And the nameless woman,
who must have a name,

once more appears.

Nightstallion

Frayed edges echo hollow
Fae's lodgers longing mooring
Among the heather and the heath
Cryptids' gurgling giggles wallow.

Barehoofed hunters luring
Prayed and preyed passengers whisper
Cupid's arrows ooze beneath
Venetian fern and fungi wait.

Darkness' fingers tumble twisting
Through Cassiopeia's starlit forehead
Sweating stars fevered frozen
Luna and Lucifer hanged in the sky.

Monkey House

Tiptoed pitter-patters behind the keyhole
Emptied chambers left moments before
Peeking Alice Hatter's wind-torn soul

Thoughts floating on simmered thought bubbles
Echoing footfalls splattered seconds ago
Pairs of hearts delt helter skelter spell troubles.

Tightrope walking lucidity this side of
consciousness.
A balancing act beneath the pink and white
pinstriped sky.

Moontides

Salty inhales meet
And gentle sighs escape.
Undulating undercurrents
Rolling
Riveting
Oyster beds below.

The waves' crisp fingers
crawl ashore.
In one huge gasp
Hold a collective breath
And exhale too slow.

Liminal Ineffability

A place that is not
Never was
And may never be.
Salt softly shaken
On this reality.

Liminality,
Neither here nor there.
A petrichor-scented grove
Of marble columns and brick.

The seasoning
Of time and trial.
Whisps of whispers,
Stampeding through moonlight
And dancing to dew.

Nomadic in nature
But comfortably
Sat in this ineffability.
Swirling memories
Clingingly clatter,
Shattering expectations' wit.

And we the culprit and the captor

Contend with the unendingness.

Peas and Cease

"Peas and cease!" she croaks,
Before hopping to a lillypad anew.

"Please and seas!" he squelched,
Crawling upon the murky lotus dew.

Why salamanders dance with letters
When reptiles cry for arms' fire clue.

The amphibians' life made senseless
When vegetation peacetalks ensue.

For frogs and lizards are foibles,
Necromancer's delightful desserts.
With tadpoles and Hawkeyes
and muddied-up footprints.

Nothing but gruesome glitter
And blood that runs thick like glue.

Sonder

I remember you at 37.
Drawing bubble letters
On welcome signs,
Garden gloves and grass stained shoes.

I remember her at 67.
Hand-quilted letters
On a blanket rack,
Thimbles, petticoats, and bowling shoes.

It's easier now to overlay us
As paper dolls,
One on top of the other,
Paper tabs grasping each other
Hugging shoulders and hips.

Santa Muerte

The corvid death doula dances
Hopping from one scraggly black leg to another
Cawing
Crowing
Beak tucked into plume'd breast.

Now, lungs expanded, throat exposed.
The oil-swilled crest expands skyward,
Squaking,
Chuckling,
"Life is still here."

Bones rattle beneath city streets
Unknown death speakers,
"Jaw bone connected to the--"
Haphazardly strewn in catacombs.

Peasant and pauper sat next to
Prince and priest.
Death makes us equal there.
But not yet.

A Walk Down 180

Witch's bells tinkle,
signifying the start.
Down, down, down
The steep steps we traverse
My pupper and I side by side

Trills from Magdalena's Notebook mingle
with operatic warmups wafting from floors
above.
Incense strains to smother pot across the lobby
As dental tools whirl and laughter rings doors
down.

Impatient clackity-clack nails dance on tile
as we leave the double doors and the 1914
building.

An olfactory buffet greets my friend.
A sensory smorgasbord of delight.
Messages upon messages left
For his and his kind's nose alone.

Snoot to the ground,
my Moz misses nothing.
We walk slowly.

Much more subdued now.
A subdivided New York Minute.

The world whooshes by,
in rapid Spanish and yammering Yiddish.
And we simply exist in it.
Content to be.

Dracaena Trifasciata

They call it mother-in-law's tongue
Do not water it too often.
Only a tablespoon will do.

If you feed the mother-in-law's tongue too
frequently, it will die.

First, it will turn vibrant green,
Then it will become transparent,
Shrivel up,
Lose its roots,
And eventually, it will no longer have any use.

Do not overwater the mother-in-law's tongue.
Only a tablespoon will do.

Do you know why?

Resplendent Komorebi

As sunlight filters through trees' filigree leaves,
Forest-crowning clouds shadowing recede.
Misted morning filaments
Upon edifice and crumbs.

A pair of pigeons' abandoned egg
Lays cracked nearby.

Artificial ancients house relics.
Frankensteinian cobbles and bricks
Combine centuries and countries
Into cloisters upon Washington's hill.

Ink

Droplets of topaz swirl with badger
making waves of light visible on paper.
Alchemy encounters reality.
Witchcraft in my small Heights kitchen.

Shaking splatters alabaster,
Starlight appears.
Memories and imaginations
Pictures set aside and dreams laid out.

Wise men emerge,
a profanity-spewing alien bird.
Anything and everything
can come forth through my fingers.

If only I can sit still.

Senbazuru Zephyr

Paper cranes and fishing line
Future stories held together by practiced fingers.
Hope, creased and folded upon the guideline.

Anchors of origami
Floating on wishes and grief
Praying for healing and respite.

A thousand colored birds strung
A thousand prayers whispered into each wing.
A unified voice pleading into every one,
"Be well. Be safe. Be sage."

Comfrey in the Heather Garden

We are the best of ourselves,
Daughters of the earth,
Here among the herbs and wildflowers
Upon the hill where Margaret Corbin is honored
"As no woman has been honored before."

The thread between a grandmother,
Mother,
And granddaughter
Who three shared existence in Her
womb for a few short months.

As I walk with my four-legged companion,
he stops to smell things I cannot see.
I try to remember things beyond the
memory of my lifetime.
We both sense outside our moment.

My sister and I,
two grown women now,
Two magical mystical moments of life and love
Who through our mother walking beside us
Once shared physical space with her mother,
gone now over a decade.

As we three walk along the Central Path,
My little black dog noses the comfrey.
A butterfly floats past and lands upon the sage.
Be safe. Be safe. Be sage.
All is well.

Sailboats on the Hudson

Paint strokes of velveteen,
Whiskey and ambered sighs,
On canvases of choppy grey macrame.

Bits and blobs of splintered boats
Peeking through hilltop trees
Sails awash in colored castaway.

Broken sidewalks head the view
Crumbling cement encores it, too.

But for two paces out of 10,000,
Sailboats on the Hudson
Come visit my dayscape land.

Rocks of Cape Ann

Recital of the rosary
Said on Mala beads of pearl.
"Mother...Mother...Mother,"
Intoned into the sea.

Fingers rubbing purposefully
Against former oyster's imperfections.
Grains of sand transformed to beauty.

Toes digging anxiously
Into wet, cold sand.

My parents.
My husband.
And me.